Prayer of the World

Prayer of the World

A Rainbow Psalm

Kathleen Maia Tapp

Earthword Press

Prayer of the World: A Rainbow Psalm

Earthword Press

Library of Congress Control Number: 2020948104

ISBN (hardcover): 9781662905636
ISBN (paperback): 9781662905643
eISBN: 9781662905650

ACKNOWLEDGMENTS

A special thanks to my husband Ken Tapp
for the majority of the photographs

Heartfelt thanks to Lynda Sacamano for support with many facets of this project, to Jesse White for design assistance, and to Marcelle Martin, Ken Jacobsen, Maggie Moon O'Neill, Marcia Tyriver, Diana Ryan, Jean Eden, and Sue Nelson, for prayerful support. Gratefully remembering Katharine Jacobsen who advocated for *Prayer of the World* in many ways. Also, a special thanks to Regina, Bev, my sisters Mary Kennedy Walker and Sister Timothy Marie, and my son Kristopher Tapp for ongoing support.

Deep gratitude and acknowledgment to the
Lyman Fund for generous support
Grateful acknowledgments to other included photographers:

Guillaume Meurice from Pexels—Page 9
Felix Mittermeier from Pexels—Page 24
James Wheeler from Pexels—Page 27
Streetwindy from Pexels—Page 33
Maggie Moon O'Neal—Page 37
Frank Cone from Pexels—Page 42
Lynda Sacamano—Pages 46, 94, 110
Tomas Malik from Pexels—Page 60
Simon Matzinger from Pixabay—Page 61
Sindre Strom from Pexels—Page 73
Dipu Shahin from Pexels—Page 88
Cottonbro from Pexels—Page 91
Luis Quero from Pexels—Page 92
Valeria Boltneva from Pexels—Page 95
Silvana Palacias from Pexels—Page 98
Jonas Von Werne from Pexels—Page 99
Sergio Omassi from Pexels—Page 101
Kristopher Tapp—Page 103
Riadh Dallel from Pexels—Page 104
Dhivakaran S. from Pexels—Page 107
Pritam Kumar from Pexels—Page 108
Suraphat Nuea-on from Pexels—Page 111
Nandhu Kumar from Pexels—Page 114
Tom Verdoot from Pexels—Page 117

Jacket photograph by Sindre Strøm
Back Cover photographs by Ken Tapp

I am the cloud
the whisper of the cloud
the changing face of the cloud

I am color   I am air

I am water
I am change

I dream
and my dreams take shape

No form holds me ....

I am Mother
and this is
the rainbow dance

This is the rainbow web

And I speak from the flower
spread   fragrant fingers
I sway as breezes blow

while my greenness reaches high
to the sky world   yellow sun   blessed Light

    as the warmth penetrates my body
    it softens, yields, surrenders

      opens

and releases its own sunburst

all is open   raining color
the whole world is color

daisy yellow   rose red   periwinkle
        pink of thistle blossom   lavender gift
                orange of nasturtium

and green   green   everywhere green
        green that gives you   life   and breath

I drink the sun

do you know the song of the scents
the healing secrets
can you let the flowers talk
can you see their open hand
take what they offer
let your eyes drink in their beauty

I am the rainbow Spirit

and you   my children
desperately need to find
color

You have lost the ability
to see my colors
You have become color blind

I am not hidden
I am splashing color
      my presence   my presents
           all over the Earth

and I call to you   see me

         OPEN YOUR EYES

"Those who have eyes to see, let them see"

I ask you to call back the rainbow
I have painted the land in rainbow song

The colors   the sounds   the presences

all form a web of life

I weave
color
I weave
life

I dance
and
weave

I sing
and
weave

and I am the world
pulsing with color

and groaning
with pain

listen,
before it is
too late

The web and the rainbow are one

You have lost your way
you have become color-blind
you do not see   my brown of Earth   yellow of sun star
                red of rose and fire   green of leaf
                blue of sky mantle   blue that deepens
                        to purple dusk

I strain to pulse life and spirit through
the dense thought mass of this flailing planet
I reach out to you   through all life   the web of life

and you do not see

I speak to you from the flowers, the leaves, the brook, the mountains and the stones of Earth; from the desert, the tundra, the cities bound in cement and plastic and reeking of fumes from your wrong life. I will even speak to you from these stuck and dangerous places although I have to push my way through cracks in your cement.

Sallow ones—for you *are* growing sallow
and losing the colors—especially the verdant green of life—
        stop   listen

        My loving energy flows toward you
        through earth and air and water
          and through you—

but you are stopping my energy
you stop the loving embrace and flow of life
      you freeze the energy
      and all comes out of balance

From the beginning time my love has flowed

I am Spirit   Ruah Greenness   Life

In the dark   fertile Earth   I am
In the delicate green tendrils of young plants
          I am

The rainbow song will lead you through the time of trouble and suffering

I flow through life in all its forms
modern people can only glimpse me sideways
        through   machines which detect energy
and through words of science
        which detect connection   and intelligence.
These methods will never detect the heart of Love
                at the center of life

Feel the heart of my life deep in the center of the planet—
    the long trail of fire in the sky that leads back, back to first Light

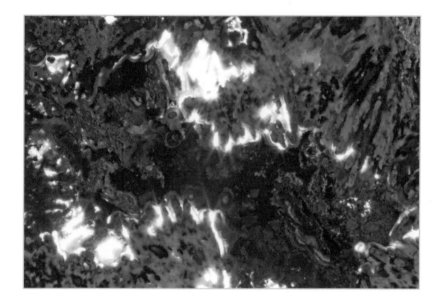

I am energy

in stone   in earth
in water   in air

and in the places *between*

where my life
strains and swells
ripples and
soars
rumbles and
flows,
churns
and
crawls,
flies and
walks,
and slides
and
glides

People of Earth   children of the rainbow
You are in a cosmic alive cocoon
and color   and song

and you do not see
you do not hear
you do not feel

and time is running out

Your world is my maypole and I weave
streamers of color around you

and yet it is all ME

For I *am* your world   I *am* your Earth and I *am* color

You must listen   the time is at hand
and I give you the gift of rainbow
A bridge through this time of storm
and trail of blood and hope

Now the green

The Earth wears a green cape   green jewels   succulent green   life

I give you green   the trees   great gnarled trunks and roots that
reach into the Earth   drinking deep waters   probing   exploring

Leaves drinking   trees breathing

I speak from the tree and I give you green
Love wears green
Love grows green

I speak from the tree
I open hands of green   I drink light   I give you air

I am the lungs of Earth
you are killing me—Earth's green

I speak from the birch, the beech, the maple, the oak, the man-grove, the eucalyptus, the great forests of evergreen, the trees of the jungles, the trees of the mountains, the trees of the plains, the trees of the great rainforests

I speak from the butterfly
No more heavy crawling   furry gobbling   hunger
the world closed-in   close-up   no view
no more the longing, unfulfilled
now the sky   now the clouds   now the soaring flight
now the time of the wings

I speak from the monarch   yes
I speak from the luna moth   yes

I am Earth   I am blue sky   I am Mother
I speak from the stars in the fiery far-off splendor
the universe is vast

I am the
delicate flower
growing by
the wayside

and I AM
the fiery star
furnace

I flow through
    the power lines
        of Earth

Spirit wanting
    release
        expression

You are my body
Earth is my body

Earth feels my pulse
you feel my pulse

I am the groaning Earth
I am your mother

The time is growing short
can you understand
can you listen
can you *attend*?

This is critical

The spirit of life infuses you   surrounds you   envelopes you
Love surrounds you   infuses you   envelopes you

I speak from the brook

I am water   splashing   caressing the stones of Earth

I carry life liquid to the plants   to the animals   to the people
I flow over stones smoothing and rounding their scars from
Earth's time of burning   I caress them cool them   love them
Love flows in this Earth that you call your own

You do not own the Earth
I flow through your body
I flow through Earth's body
you poison your body
you poison Earth's body
heal your body
heal Earth's body

the jewel is dimming
    scarring   filling with poison

I speak from the stone
I carry healing energy
      the love, the energy of
Earth
the forces that burst from the stars
are held in the nuggets   stones
     star "magic"

all connected in a web of life

Song

Breath

Energy

Praise

It is the time of the butterfly   rainbow butterfly

You must rise up

You are still young and foolish
and the hills are watching
they do not clap their hands
they watch in horror
they brace themselves on their foundations of rock
they call for help from the deepest Source

I am the Mother
I flow through the veins of mountains
I call to you from the hills and valleys
        from the rivers and seas
I call to you from the starry skies

The stars are preparing…
unless you join Earth's prayer
unless you let the song of life
flow through you and through the land
there will be a darkness

And so I speak from the sun
the great firelight of this system
hearth-fire
legendary god
flame furnace
I speak heat   light   life
I shine
My being leaps in flame webs that spark
and sizzle and scorch
and kill and heal
    and give you your life on Earth

I will teach you how to pray

This book is the prayer of the world

I call to you from the voice of wind
I flow to you   on currents of air
I am the flow   halo   light   air
          prayer of the wind

All is connected in a
living breathing web
and I am the web
the living pulse of energy
that flows through all creation
each pulse a prayer

love prayer in birdsong
leafing branch-ways
foaming surf
scudding clouds
wheeling planets

All around you lies the prayer of life—

I pray the Earth into being
I sing the Earth   spring   flow   into being
I dance the Earth   its life   into being
join the prayer
the web is hugely strained
growing more feeble

I am Lace-maker   web of life

Prayer of the World

My love streams from the stars
springs from the Earth
flows from the waterfall
reaches up in green shoots
    and rainbow blossoms   seeking sky

My love infuses all
        sends healing essences through the web
            the strained web

The world is a visible manifestation of my love

    You must open your eyes and hearts

My love for you creates the prayer of the world

The Earth is my prayer of love

Love flows through your own body
bring it—and you—to time of bloom
Love flows through Earth's body
bring it to time of bloom

this is a rainbow psalm

I am your mother
I smile and say your name
I am with you
you have work to do—

to reach deep within yourself
the kingdom within
and find the buried treasure
          to pour forth
     My presence in the world

Nest

Consider the bird   how she begins to weave and build
  until she has formed a receptacle   a nest
                              a place for the egg

and she will tend the nest
and she will tend the egg
          cover it   with her body   keep it warm   keep it safe

consider that   then
something new is born
and in the birthing
the egg cracks,
breaks into many pieces
and disappears

and the nest   holds firm
   a place of warmth and safety for the new creature
it will continue to be the part of the Earth
that the bird knows as home

until the bird learns to use its wings

and then   what of the nest?
what happens to the weaving of twigs and grasses and leaves?

Slowly   gradually it returns to Earth
and the Mother knows that its time
for housing her young one is over
She will build another one when the
time is ripe
   nests do not last through winter's gales

and all that is left is a soft memory
        in the tree   in the bird
           in the Earth

Nests   there are many kinds of weavings and gatherings and
buildings of home places   the web of life holds many nests,
burrows, homes for creatures   places where they feel held

Civilization itself is a nest

built by much weaving   working building tending
and there have been many hatchings   many young ones
swooping, feeding, flying, leaving

but nests serve their purpose and return to nature
they recycle into the web
it would be futile for the ragged interlacings
of twig and weed to try to hold back nature's rhythm and plan
       They surrender
and in that surrender, they contribute to the next phase
and the Mother will keep weaving   gathering   tending

There will be new nests   new seasons   new birth

       ***softness* ....**

We need to soften sharp angles and texture and ways
      and remember   *softness*

**The softness of
the open heart**

*Then you will see the colors of my
Rainbow   Spirit   Song*

Hatchings are sometimes very hard   very difficult

sometimes the breaking of a shell is painful
           one feels jabbed by the broken bits
                      wobbly   unsure
sometimes   it takes time to find and use the wings

one wishes to fly back to the nest
even after learning flight
one does not want to see the lacework
    of the nest fall into disrepair

because   *what then*?

Where does one go
if one is used to going "back"

Now the only way is forward
                    with new wings

Forward into the blue sky   green trees   humming life
          yellow of new morning

One needs then   more than ever
                    the song of the colors

Eagle and Turtle

The eagle flies high in the sky   with great power
The turtle moves in slow plodding earthbound steps

The turtle is Earth

The eagle is sky

I am the Mother
I speak from the eagle
I speak from the turtle

Listen to both

And the cross—the intersection of Earth and sky
where slow plodding earthbound creatures
meet the one who soars freely in the sky kingdom
that is the cross

Turtle—slow   old   wise   hiding sometimes in a ponderous shell
does turtle dream of lightness of being?
does turtle wish for wings?

Turtle's view is earthbound
Turtle knows how gravity
    holds one down
Turtle knows water
gliding sliding into silk of
water

Eagle knows space   height
            freedom
Eagle does not feel bound by gravity
Eagle's view is immense   majestic
Eagle feels the exhilarating rush of wind holding her up
bearing her along in the upper reaches of sky

Does eagle wonder how life
feels for those limited earth-
bound creatures
scurrying below?
Does eagle wonder
how life would feel
beneath a shell
of armor?

And the cross
     where Earth meets sky
         where limits of gravity-bound life, the armored life
         meet the freedom, the vistas, the soaring life   the sky

Turtle—slow, old, wise creature of the web
Eagle—fast, sky-bound creature of the web
two teachers
and when the energy of turtle meets the energy of eagle
at that intersection   is the place of possibility
                  and dream and shift   to new life

That point of intersection is surrounded   enveloped by a circle
the circle of compassion

open heart

People of Earth

Turtle energy is out of balance   your armored shell grows thicker,
denser, heavier, more clumsy, burdensome   while the creature
within the shell—once and sometimes known for wisdom—is shriv-
eling, sinking beneath the heavy weight, and soon all will be shell

Can you even look up?   Now at this critical point in time
in history?
Can you perceive eagle?

Can your weak and
dimming eyesight
find the   possibilities
of a being who surmounts
the world of heavy gravity

    and learns to fly

when you can let the energy of eagle
infuse the overly-armored   lumbering place
where you stand and totter
then you will begin to know the cross

what it means while still a creature of Earth
to find the deep space of possibility within and without
the great expanses   for you were *made* to find the greatness

There is an immense inner sky
where your spirit longs to roam
in this immense inner sky
              is your home

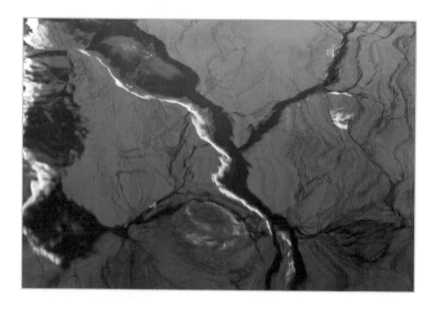

When you find the inner sky
and your spirit can shed the armor that has become far too heavy
for your frame and your life
then   there   in that vibrant fully alive space where Earth meets sky
       you will also feel the circle around you
            the web of all life
         My Presence   My   love

For I am turtle
and I am eagle

I speak from the turtle   I speak from the eagle

I speak from the circle   the web
    the   Heart of Love

the vast fount of love
joins the creatures of Earth

There are many more citizens of Earth than you recognize
You see the tree   the bark   the leaf   the branch   the blossom
You do not see soul
You do not know all there is to know about
the tree   bush   flower   bud

I am the Mother and I speak through the Earth
I pour myself out into the beings and presences of Earth
for the green world is dear to many beings   and in your arrogance
you are affecting destinies of beings all
around you   and from many realms

The Earth is in pain
She is a being
and time is running out
Listen   to the story of   Earth   stone   tree
The stories flow through channels like rivers

Some bends in this river speak through folklore and legends
and some speak through the words of science
it is a rich kaleidoscope   how my colors woven through the world
carry threads of story   legend   and myth   *and a larger truth*

The tales of humankind approach great truths and then reel back
and label them for children, for the imagination of the young.

Stone

The mountains know my name   I speak through the mountains
   through the stories of these lofty souls

Long ago before the mind of man evolved   before any form
evolved   there was a great heaving and crashing and spewing   a
fiery tempest wrinkles forming   in Earth's agitated being.

Firestorms raged and the Earth vomited molten flows toward the sky
and then   the flows cooled   and the wrinkles and ridges became
rigid
and water dripped through crevices and great forms dripped into
being.

We know these caverns that hold the story of Earth's infancy

We know the stories held in the crusted fist of Earth

We, too, hold energy   light   form
Within us   the energy of the stars

Energy   light   life

Your own bodies hold
    patterns of energy
you must look within
these locked places
things are not
just as they seem

We are the locked mysterious castles of the tales you learned as
children some described as glass mountains, with sheer and glassy
slopes, impossible to scale.   These tales both give and hide great
truths

We are the castle of treasure
crystal knowing
and we are trying
    to reach you   teach you

The light streams down
from sun, our star

We know how to hold and carry
the energy and wisdom of that Light
We are ancient beings   we know the stars
All is energy   vibration   emanating from love

I am the Mother and I speak from the crystal stones

I speak through the rainbow of color
    that dances within their glassy form
they hold my energy
they hold knowledge   and healing

And you—
men and women of Earth
must open the locked places
of your own heart and history
in order to feel the life
locked within our form

The rainbow lies within us

within you

and within the time called future

The stars hold stories for you
the stars send you help
the stars are watching:

we are aware, alive
we watch in horror
            the events of Earth
                the people of Earth

the stars are preparing ...

I wear a crown of stars
I speak from the stars

I am the Mother

In the space between your thoughts
                    I am
In the space between the molecules of your physical body
                    I am
In the space between the rocks
          where green tendrils of wild plant reach for life
                    I am
I dance between the forms

          and in the space between the time of destruction
          and the dawn of a new time   a new story

                    I am

I am the Mother
I speak from the beings
   of the cave and rock
they are part of my Presence
           on this Earth

listen—
   Open your ears, your hearts

We implore the humans of Earth
to pull back, reconsider,
use the brains for which
their species is known

use it to gain understanding
not to amass wealth
use it to strengthen and
help heal the web
instead of destroying it

to unite intellect and heart
so that you can see   hear
understand   and   feel

before it is too late

In stories thought to be for children,
the cave holds jewels   treasures
there are words to open the secret door

there are locked places on Earth that hold treasures of spirit
there are locked places in the human heart
that hold treasures of spirit

there are ways to open locked places
the power of the word

    I am love
    I open locked places
    and the colors pour through
    like life-giving streams

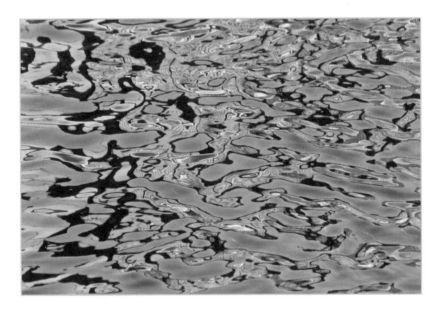

Green   rainbow   moon   Mary
  Wisdom Sophia Guadalupe Lourdes Fatima
            White Buffalo Calf Woman
                 Tara   Quan Yin
                      Shakti

Pray   Raise the vibration
there is a unity
that you do not   cannot   see
        or understand

there is a beautiful lacework
of connecting threads
energies of all beings
that form a pattern that is
beautiful   elegant
            holy

I take you deeper into green ....

green   of jade   tourmaline   emerald
green of algae   moss   lichen
new leaf
new life

"I am the vine
you are the branches"

I will take you even deeper into green
down the worn steps of stone,
steps now covered with lichen and moss

I speak from the stone

I remember Earth's beginning time
I know the fire   the stars
the far-flung spiral dance of creation
Humans have scratched their symbols
on my skin
I am the historian of Earth
stories swirl through my veins
    the green life of story

   I am the Mother and I *care*
   I want to protect my children
     to hold all beings safely
   in my web of life   and love
   I want to cover all of you
   with my mantle

I want to weave the rainbow psalm and song
   through   your days   your life   your world

I take you deeper into blue …

Mysterious blue
the depths of pools—
pools of the Earth
      pools of the eyes

What do you know of blue?
You see the blue sky   blue sea
    but you
do not see

The sky
ripples blue
and I speak
from the sky
the sea
churns blue
and I speak
from the sea
the
inner self knows blue   and I speak to your deepest soul
                  and I speak through you

I gather you in blue
I stretch the silk of blue
across the top of the world
I pour blue into the
      cup of the globe

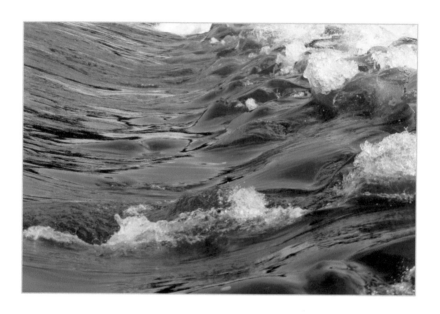

I sing blue
and my song spins
a mantle
and yes   yes   yes
I cover you in blue

Peacock

Consider the peacock
how he struts
how he spreads his many-feathered splendor

how each feather holds rainbow sheen   blue mystery
how he shows those feathers   archway of rainbow
at the time of new life

The peacock holds this rich promise all his life
much of the day he is unaware—
eating, sleeping, surviving
but the feathers hold their own memory and promise
they help the peacock to go beyond survival
and for moments of vibrant quivering intense rainbow
he is fully radiantly alive
he is feather   color   pulse of life
he stands differently on the Earth
fills the space with energy
fulfills his promise

What time do *you* now stand in?
        what promise, potential
                do you stand ready to enfold
                        children of Earth

In the time of my rainbow song
   there are many teachers
I speak through those teachers.
Some stand on two legs
   some stand on four
some swim   some fly
some you do not see at all
but they watch over you
with love
and mounting concern

Donkey

Consider the donkey   how he moves   slowly
deliberately   with plodding steps
consider his unassuming color   gray to brown
he has a stubborn will   a determined gait
consider how time enfolds the donkey in its stories
       how mystery can touch those with plodding gait
        whose eyes are so often fixed on the ground

Consider the stories——
    Who the donkey carried on his back
      his hide like a nest   his slow steps in that moment
      becoming like the winged messenger Being

Consider how majesty and mystery can kiss the one
whom others feel have no destiny or mission
The donkey's back carried the sacred story

The donkey's steps knew the path toward birth
Death   mystery   and again   *new life*

Consider the donkey
all you who feel that your vision holds no glory
your eyes can see no farther than the ground right by your feet
who feel vulnerable, unprotected, plodding—
for you also hold in your bodies the life of brown
                    and your steps know the path

Wheat

Consider the wheat   how it grows tall under the summer sun
how the wind sends the chaff blowing through the air   how the
kernels of goodness fill the farmer's bin   release their form as they
are ground to flour's softness again release their form   to become
bread   many types of bread   many shapes of bread   many fla-
vors of bread   for many bakers of bread   in many lands

the energy of sun   green life   remains
through all the changes and transformations
the kernel   the flour   the bread   hold the vital life force

many elements have shared their gifts   many people have con-
tributed their labor   and in the end product   the wheat does not
recognize itself at all
        its part in the web of life is huge
        it receives from the web
                it yields   it transforms
                it gives back to the web

Listen to the story of the wheat kernel
And be attentive to the places of hard kernels within
Where goodness must be ground, open, cracked
        to release gifts   to the web of life

I am the Mother

I am the white light
and when I reach to Earth
        I bend   I swirl   I dance
        and in the bending and dancing
        I am in that moment—prism
        and I pour myself forth
        green of growing things
        blue of sky dome   yellow of sun
        brown of Earth   rich and fertile
        silver of the shining web of spider
           teacher of weaving and lacework

People of Earth   children
      look up   look down   look within
       the rainbow swirls within you also
       the green of life's vitality
         yellow of sun-warmth
       blue calm of the deep lake on a windless day
      brown   gray   you are of the clay

I give you brown I give you Earth

Earth is MY body
and I speak from the Earth

Jewels lie within
jewel of thirsty root
sparkling gem
dripping cavern
soft burrow
and fire
deep within

The rivers pour blood through veins of brown
    clouds   release raindrops
        that   darken Earth to rich black loam
                Queen of jewels

            Queen who tends the hot fire
                    Who   knows brown   knows green
                    knows how brown gives life to green
                        which rises toward blue
                            and sends seeds   back   to   brown

I am brown   I am Earth
              I speak from the Earth

I have been violated
my skin opened and scraped

my jewels taken and sold
        jewels of   gem   seed   water   plant   creature

my river veins poisoned
the burrows destroyed

and even the stones are stunned

What happens when brown loses itself
its rich fertile deep life?
What happens when brown grows pale
and dry and caked
or wet and foul

I am uneasy
the rhythm falters

My heartbeat   my pulse   sustains all

the winds rise and move across the Earth
        following the rhythm   the pulse
the seas churn   roll   curl and   foam
        following the rhythm   the pulse
the trees drink light   breathe for the globe
        following the rhythm   the pulse

Listen to
the alarm cries
of the birds

the animals

the foreboding voice of the storm rising from hot Earth

I am Mother
it is the time of rainbow
I would gather you all under my mantle
I would stretch it across the sky
         to cover you
         and keep you safe

We have sung of the blue   the green   the brown
                 sky   plant   Earth
     And what of fire?   red   orange   yellow fire ....

I am star
I am fire   and light
I sing across cold space   I dance fire

and the flame lines of my dance
        touch Earth   ignite green life
            and leave you wondering
        who I am   and how my   fiery story
        fits with yours
        and how these web lines
        connect to story
    in the vastness of space

        and do these burning orbs
        connect with others
        and do they form a shape
        and do they tell a story
        and all the while
            I burn   I dance
            I sing fire and light

I am Mother   I speak from the star
the stars call out your name
the stars   my light
the stars   my fire
the stars sing light and fire

the love   the pulse   the flame
of my fire hurtles through space
to form a dome of blue
to begin the gentle breath   of life   on Earth

My children, the time of the rainbow is upon you
whirling dancing colors that send their life
          upon a tortured Earth   a struggling people.
          You must open your eyes
                    your heart   before it is too late

"those who have eyes to see   let them see ..."

Rose

And softly   I speak of the rose—
layers of petals   soft and gentle
        I am the rose

Can you glimpse the heart that
beats at the hidden core
beyond the unfolding petals
which both reveal
            and conceal
            the beauty of the rose

Mother love
You will see me everywhere
   if your eyes are open

I am the rose
I am softness   beauty
Mystery that opens in layers
of time and space
Mystery that glows from hidden corners
from the highest spires   hills   cathedrals
Mystery that winds itself
amidst the green in wayside paths

Mystery that
shows its face
when the sun pours
out its light

I am the Mother
I speak from the rose
Listen ...
can you feel the
rainbow forming above you   below you   through you
can you sense the strands of blue   green   yellow orange   red
and beyond the spectrum of expectations
the brown   the silver   the pink

can you feel the dance
the pulse of rainbow
arching through space
   through Earth
   through you?

The light of love
bends through the prism
of itself
and pours down color

I know white
smooth white of egg
which does not stay
still and silent
but begins to move,
rock   make noise
and then finds its
world cracking
and all is move-
ment   stretch
and new color
the white has
birthed newness
from within itself

I know white

the white of   moon
which does not stay
static and still
in the heavens
but grows night by night
swelling like an
expectant mother
from crescent to quarter
to half to full circle
of shining white
and all the while
    traveling the sky

the whiteness glows   grows
cracks   hatches
waxes   wanes   shines

I am the Mother
I speak through white
I give you white
I enfold you in love

And I speak from the wind:
north wind   south wind   east wind   west wind

    I am wind
    I rise from the Earth
    I breathe it into being
    and the Earth breathes me
    into being

    wind of Earth's breath
    wind of your spirit
        my breath
    breathing you into life
      breathing you into yourself

I am the Mother   I speak from the wind

I am water
I have served you well
I have filled your streams
rivers and oceans
given homes to fish dolphins
sharks   whales
crabs and seaweed
seals and sand creatures

I am water
I drip through crevices
and my drip
becomes rock
I flow over stones in
creeks and rivers
and the rocks
become   smooth
in tongues of foam I speak

I am raindrop
but something is wrong
My liquid self is one with poison
I pour poison on the land
and I am my own teardrop

I am water
I cannot hold the
boundaries
   of my self
I cannot protect
my filmy skin
And I am in Earth
   in those who walk with
two legs and four legs
and those who crawl
   and those who fly
I make up the seas within you
   the seas that hold
   the salt of the ocean
The inner seas   the outer seas

The seas that now hold poison

I am the Mother

Listen   *Respond*

I am Earth   I pulse life
but the rhythm falters
the heartbeat is strained
distress trickles down
with the poison

and some of the beings
who walk my soil
    and fly my skies
    and swim my seas
        are gone now

distress trickles deeper
I grind my teeth
and plates shift
and mountains rumble
and the seas rear
pawing the sand with foam
spitting out poison

I am the Mother
I speak from   storm and wind and cloud
    and rain and sea
  heaving   pawing   simmering one

I am the fierce love
the pulse that pounds
and swells
and cracks and opens
and rains and blows
and all is movement

the rhythm gathers
  the wrongness
and rears up

My people
        you are part of the great pulse and heartbeat

      You have a part to play in this time of rainbow

the stars   my burning eyes   send you light
weave webs of light across the firmament
the sun   my face   sends   life and warmth
the moon   my night face   sends you white hope
visions of change
calls your tides   sings with your seas
within   without—

for within you lies the light of the sun and moon and stars
within you the song of the sea   pulse of the tides
rhythm of the green life

        within you the stone and star
        the water and the salt of rock
        clay of Earth
        within you the pain pulse
        that shudders the mountain

and now   within you   the poison

RISE UP!

Strengthen the web

I am the web
join your prayers
with mine
  the green life
of your soul

 your prayers joining
 and connecting
 around the globe
  will help to   heal the web
hear me
I am the Mother
I am the web
I speak from Earth
her pain and
  her promise
Reach for the colors

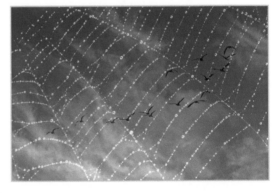

they are within
they are without

your prayers are a vital part
of the pulse of life

They hold power to heal
　　to join with me
　　　in a rainbow psalm

Pray the green   the blue   yellow orange   red   fire
　　　　　the white   the brown
　　　　　　　the   silver   web

Water Lily

Consider the water lily   delicate and strong   it floats upon the
face of the water   yet sends its greenness down to anchor in Earth
it is a circle of welcome for small creatures   their resting place
where water meets sun   it turns its face   to the light   floating
with the water pulse and current

It knows color
    pink like sunset
        that blooms upon the water
    pink like clouds
        that float upon the water

water lily gives the gift of one who never loses anchor—never is lost—
yet knows how to gracefully surrender
and   while holding so artfully the tension
        between roots and freedom ... *blooms*

Pink—
the pearly sheen of the conch
pink luster   listening ear

pink   the color of new life

pink   scared to move
          eager to move
the tender place
of the unguarded heart

when the world presses in on the new one's pink tenderness
it feels the hardships   the hate   the scorn of others
it begins to grow plates of armor

and when the flow of time itself becomes
a difficult birth tunnel
          new ones emerge   pink   and   vulnerable
          then will come the time of pink
                    its glory   its potential

It is the task of a lifetime
to preserve the pink of the young vulnerable one
through the hardships of life

Unless you can reach that pink softness
that dares to be open and vulnerable
you will not find the freedom
of your own inner sky

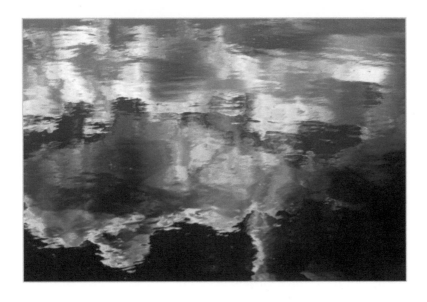

The heart's armor blocks the gate

men   women   children of Earth
there is much to mourn
much has been lost
many beings in the web of life
   have been killed   maimed   silenced
many of my children are hungry and sick
do not armor your hearts against their suffering
do not wrap yourself in coverings
   so you do not see them
hear them   know them

Pink calls to you
from within   from without

I am pink
the tightly furled pink of rosebud
the rose at the center of the heart

I am the Mother
I call to you from the pink heart
the newborn groping pink ones
I call to you from the future
from the time yet to come—
                the emerging time of pink

Prayer is the lifeblood of the web

Prayer energizes all
Prayer helps you remove
   your over-armored burden
and reach for the inner sky
Prayer helps to weave the threads
of the rainbow bridge
between the inner world
        and the outer world
and   know they are but different aspects
            of the *same* world

Prayer is the water trickling through crevices in rock
Prayer is the sea wave breaking on the shore
        and changing a whole landscape

Prayer is the voice of the land

In true prayer you soften
the hard kernel
which holds back
the delight of the colors—
the living grace
of the green world
the endless blue freedom
of sky
the hope of the rising sun
the pulse of brown earth
that pulse reflecting
through all beings

Listening is prayer

when the hard kernel
that fortresses the heart
begins to soften
    that is prayer

when the softening heart
hears the faint
far-off sound
unfamiliar—
the gasp of the Earth

    that is prayer

and when the heart
has opened enough
that its perception shifts
and it senses it does not live through its own strength
alone, but is held in a web of life
       supported by the earth   air   water   sun
       other beings
         the Ground of all being   the Mother—

    that is prayer

and in the opening, the
heart is a water lily
knowing itself in a land-
scape of fluid life
opening its bloom of color
yet anchored to the solid Earth

    that is prayer

The human heart holds
the vastness of the cosmos
one can spend a lifetime
listening
     softening   opening

the embrace of the open heart
     touches all

and the softness begins
to shimmer—
take on the sparkle of a web
in the morning mist
connecting with
everything   everyone
and even then
the opening is not completed—

for the heart
now listening intently
feeling the throb
and beauty of life
begins to sing
     the colors

And that is love

Some scorn the peacock   call it foolish   proud
they say it struts and preens and is a silly animal
they do not know how the world feels to peacock
the peacock feels its world to be the most important of all creatures

In the time when new life is being created   the peacock calls
forth the rainbow   and some might say even then that he is a silly
bird and vain   but he is doing his best   raising the colors of the
rainbow the only way he knows   in his part to help bring new life
into being

and in that exhilarating moment,
the feathers, which are the brown
of Earth
catch the transforming fire
of the sun
and become rainbow

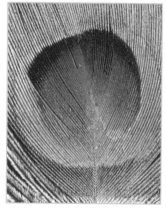

    and that is prayer

And then there is the donkey who some call stubborn. They do not know how the world feels to the donkey  how loads can be heavy and terrain rough, life sometimes cruel and yet the donkey knows that in the story of his kind there are tales of wonder and greatness, that those of his kind have gone beyond the drudgery, the familiar burdens—and reached true glory. Songs are sung of those times— and stories are told of the donkey's greatness

And in the daily plodding, in the feeling of burden and fear and weight, in the drudgery and struggle and rocky terrain—know that you carry the sacred story on your back

and that is prayer

Listen to peacock's teaching   listen deeply
move beyond doubts of foolhardiness and vanity in yourself or
your people
move beyond criticism   do not judge all movements as strutting
do not judge a show of color as vanity

The survival time of a species   calls
forth rainbows   at many levels

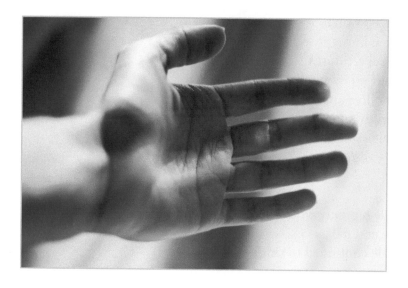

And if these words and ideas sound as unreachable and hard to
touch
as a far-off rainbow arching in the sky   know this—
the blue sky of the inner kingdom lies within your heart
the green life is within your cells and all around you on Earth
the yellow sun calls forth the fire within you
the pulse of brown earth beats beneath your feet

Whale

Consider the whale
king of the waters
singer most royal

for eons whale has sung
in deep waters
When humans were
fearful creatures
crouched by small
campfires and
primitive dwellings
whale's song filled
    the sea

while human civilizations
rose and fell
whale continued to sing

now humans are beginning to listen to the song of the whale
to reach out   understand   communicate
to see the whale with new eyes
hear with new ears
          and this is prayer

I am the Mother
and I speak from the whale
        Listen   *Respond*

And I sing from all the beings of Earth—
birds and bears and cats and dogs
and whales and butterflies and snakes
   and woodpeckers and tigers

The creatures who lived in ages past   speak to you
through the imprints they left in the rocks

The fuels you reach for so greedily
speak to you also   of a young time on the Earth
when the richly green plants
drank the sun   stored its life
then   form changed   and changed again
now you reach into the veins where Earth
stores pockets of long-ago sun life
                    a gift from the past
and you take and you do not give back

it is part of the web   a web that reaches back
to primeval days   and into the future

in your grasping   you take from the past
   and you take from the future
   and the web is greatly strained

yet the whale still sings—

I speak from the whale
I sing in dark waters

and I am dolphin
and dog
I help those whose eyes have failed
                      ears have failed
                      limbs have failed

I help you search
    have you enlisted my help in the *right* searches?

And I speak from the howl of the wolf
the slap of the beaver's tail   a warning
the dance of the bee   a tale of honey

Do you hear the call of the geese in fall
the language of the gorilla   chimpanzee
the whistle of the dolphin?

The creatures in the web speak
I say to those who listen—
            this is prayer
a glint of rainbow
I am the Mother
I speak through all the creatures
      Listen and respond

Pray the living breathing prayer
of the human person
reaching out not
as lord and ruler
but *in relationship*

            with other beings

Reach out your hand
join hands

give back to the web

add your voice to the song—

this is prayer

For long ages you have not
　　listened to the animals
for long ages you have not
　　listened to each other

the rich disregard
the words of the poor
as they disregard
the song of the whale

listen from the open heart
which has softened the hard kernel—
that wall of protection
that keeps you in a barren world
filled with things that comfort the body
but strangle and estrange the soul

All is out of balance
teetering
the nerves of the planet
are frayed

the followers of
the prophets
are warring
the people are in pain
the people
are hoarding riches
the people are starving
the Earth is a tower
of Babel

and shifting winds
    tug at the nest …

Listen to one another
Listen from the place of open heart

"on Earth as it is in heaven"

in the nest of the open heart
   your eyes will clear
you will *see* each other

see the vulnerable heart
beneath the shell
see the tender pale place
the sun has not touched

     I am the Mother
     I speak through the vulnerable ones—

Shell

The shells are many and varied
    yet are the same—
the shell of the one who governs the land
the shell of the one who carries out the law of the land
the shell of the one who makes weapons to kill those outside the land
the shell of the one who reports the events of the land
the shell of the one who sells items to the people

  the one who entices people
  to buy the items
  and the ones who choose the items
  and the ones who have no funds
  and the ones who loan the funds
  and the hungry ones who watch it all
  and the ones who denounce seller
    buyer lender enticer

the shells are different some thicker
denser more impenetrable
some woven
with weft of fear
some with rage
some with sorrow

yet beneath all shells
crouch creatures
blinking in the light
seeking comfort
assurance love

Your hearts and souls
are starving
and the bodies
of the rich
swim through deep pools
 of spangled goods
while the bodies
 of the poor sicken and die—

What gives comfort and nourishment to the soul
is not glittering goods
it is connection   many-layered connection
          with life   with other beings   with the web
            I am the web
                connect with Me

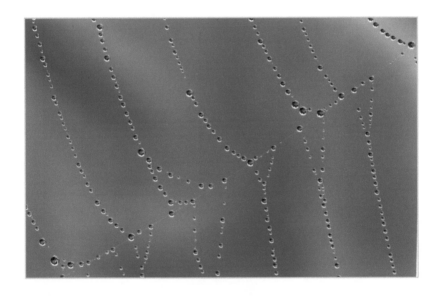

            for I am your Mother
            and I reach out to you
            through all of life

                and that is prayer

I reach out in love
Love is a word you have put in service
domesticated, like your animals
the meaning thinned   confused

but love   real love
is wild greenness   burning flame
that you will spend a lifetime discovering

Love is the heart's response—listening to the conch shell of the
world

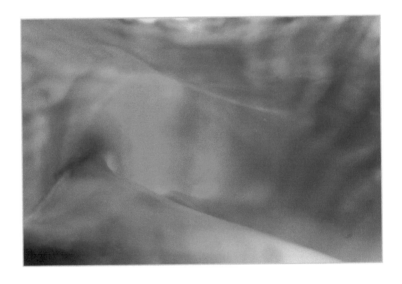

Love is the green heart   that hears the song
and sees the colors
and burns

Love is the flame of the Mother

I am the flame
alive   leaping   dancing
        searing

until all things
trivial are burned
away in love's
transforming fire—

leaving the gold nugget
        of the heart

can
the rose and the flame be one?

Yes
I speak from the flame   the blossom
at the heart of love

Ancestors

The web of life reaches across time
to those who have gone before you
         your ancestors are not gone
         they are watching over you

so many of the young ones
     are not told the stories
they do not know
who the ancestors were

and they do not know
that the ancestors'
presence remains.
they do not know
the stories of their elders

that loss is part of the grief held
in the walled fortress of
your   heart

if you have not been
told the stories
of your own family   your people
     those who came before you
how can you give the stories
     to those who come after you—
the descendants

you need the soul food
the green life of your own stories

I am the Mother
I speak through the stories of your lives
I speak through the descendants
who will come after you
I speak now through your children—

We are the children
we feel the faltering
        rhythm
    we are losing our stories
    we are losing our way
    the compass is breaking

    it grows hard to breathe

our bodies need food
    with life's vital energy
our souls need food
    with spirit's vital energy
our bodies and souls need
        green life
    story   connection
        the love
            of the web

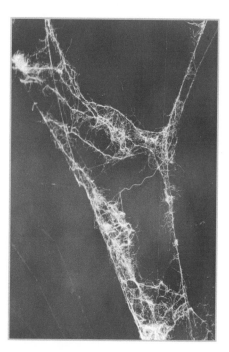

give us the rainbow
give us the map
 toward rainbow
        inner   outer
        give us life
help us to know the Mother

I am the Mother
and I speak from
    the children
who have grown
  sallow and afraid
    Listen   Respond

It   is not easy   it is not   impossible   it is not too late

Parents and teachers play games
      where children find what is hidden
play a new game   a lifelong game
help the children find the colors
     and they will help all of you
      all of Earth   weave   the rainbow

Look into another's eyes

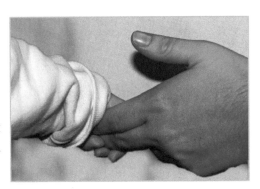

when you reach out a hand
you are like the sun
igniting green life in the heart
that huddles beneath the shell

and that is prayer

You are not alone

the web of life holds strands of pure light
that you cannot see with your physical eyes
filaments of sacred energy from sacred beings
you are more loved than you know
you are more protected and cared for than you know

imagine this web with strands of pure light
imagine the one who weaves such a web
       I am the Mother
       I speak through
     the holy ones   angel beings   bright spirits

And when you have removed the armor
that weights your heart
then you will find your way to your inner sky
    and know the bright ones who love you

when you quiet your mind   and   pray
you enter the great freedom of that blue sky within

You hold the song of the sun and stars
in your bodies are wheeling centers of energy
that reflect the rainbow colors

The hand reaching out   *that is prayer*

the hands connecting   *that is the web*
                    help one another

this rainbow web
    is strengthened subtly
hand by hand   heart by heart
        prayer by prayer

the time is now   do not wait
do not say   first I must
    finish my plan and schedule
for the nest of twigs blows away
  in the wind and chill of winter
the nest that you have built
  as a people is fragile
and the web is greatly strained
  and the Earth shudders

reach within   reach without

            listen   soften   open
        reach out   connect   care

And in that place of deepest opening   softening   listening
we come to the color of which I have not spoken—

purple   a place of healing

the flowers give us healing lavender
the stones give us healing amethyst
the sky gives us the last ribbon of sunset
before it meets the mystery of night

and your own inner skies
also hold purple's mystery
its silence   its prayer
I am purple   I speak from the edge of the twilight
          the edge of the rainbow
          the edge of your knowing

can you meet me in the
deepest silence
      of your soul?

          I am purple
          I hold out my hand
            Listen   Respond

Canary

and so we come to the canary
the canary is a teacher who has been
given the hardest job—
to lay down his life for others

The canary sits in caves where people
gather fuels   nuggets
        Earth treasures
and the canary   the delicate one
who can feel wrongness so quickly if
the air has become poisoned
absorbs the poison and dies

and his death is a warning to the people that the air is toxic

So it is that the canary's greatest gift
is in the stilled song   the silence

I am the Mother   I speak from the canary   small creature the
color of the sun

the sun who gives you life and health
the canary who warns you that health and life
are in jeopardy

the canary's gift is final

STOP THE POISON

I speak from the canary's silence
and the silence of stilled songs
creatures quietly fading from the web
a silence that looks at you with vanished eyes
and speaks to you
as do the children

they know
of the canary
they do not
want *their* gift
to be the
stilled song

They want life!

TURN BACK
FROM THE
PRECIPICE

grasp the strands of rainbow
and pull yourselves back
now

Help the Mother rebuild the nest
help the Mother weave the colors
send out prayer filaments from your heart

let the song of the bright canary
and the song of the web
speak of yellow sunrise not death
let it hold the fiery strength of yellow sun
rising toward a new dawn   a new day

and this is prayer

the prayer of the Mother

Prayer of the World

For when one truly lets go
softens the hard kernel
there is a feeling like falling
        and one is caught by the net
        the web of life

    and I am the web

    in the opening and the falling
        you fall into my arms
                and that is love

CPSIA information can be obtained
at www.ICGtesting.com
Printed in the USA
BVHW020105111221
623634BV00019B/3